The **COLORS** of MACKINAC ISLAND

JENNIFER POWELL

FOR OWEN & MAXEN

The Colors of Mackinac
Copyright 2015 © Jennifer Powell

Published by

Thunder Bay Press
Holt, MI 48842

ISBN: 978-1-933272-49-8
Library of Congress Control Number: 2015930376

Photography by Jennifer Powell.
Book & Cover Design by Julie Taylor.

Printed in the United States of America by Versa Press.

ROYGBIV

The rainbow is made up of seven individual colors, which we remember with this special acronym: ROYGBIV. Each letter represents a color: **RED, ORANGE,** YELLOW, **GREEN, BLUE, INDIGO,** and **VIOLET.**

BROWN is a combination of these colors. **GRAY, BLACK,** and WHITE can make these colors darker or lighter.

All of these colors can be found on Mackinac Island!

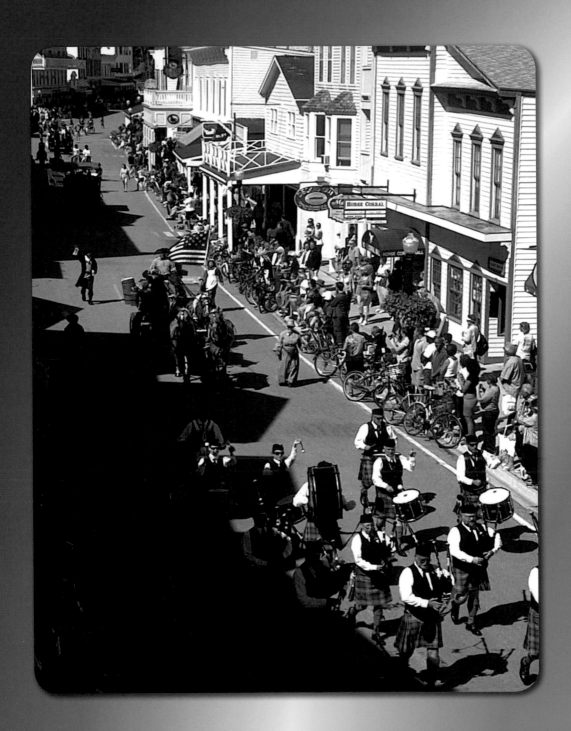

There are many different colors on Mackinac Island.

Come explore the Island and see how many you can find!

RED

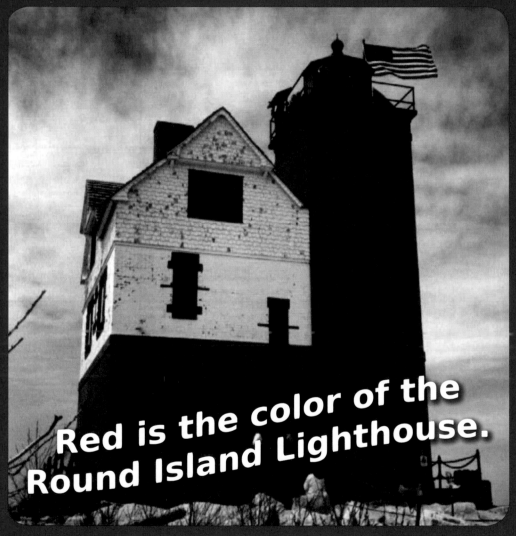

Red is the color of the Round Island Lighthouse.

It greets ferry boats as they enter the harbor.

Red is the color of the 2,500 geraniums

...that line the porch of Grand Hotel.

Red is the color of carriage wheels.

Carriages take people on tours of the Island.

ORANGE

Orange is the color of the sunset

...reflected in the waters around Mackinac Island.

Orange is the color of the Tiger Longwing Butterfly

...found in the two butterfly conservatories on Mackinac Island.

Orange is the color of the pumpkins

...that make fall festive on Mackinac Island.

YELLOW

Yellow is the color

of the Swallowtail Butterfly

...found on Mackinac Island in the summer.

Yellow is the color of the Tea Room umbrellas

...that shade the diners at Fort Mackinac.

Yellow is the color of many Island tulips.

40,000 bulbs are planted at Grand Hotel.

GREEN

Green is the color of the grass in Marquette Park.

It is a favorite spot to rest and play.

Green is the color of the stables

...that house the horses and carriages.

Green is the color of the drays pulled by horses.

Garbage is separated for either recycling or landfill before the dray takes it away.

BLUE

Blue is the color of the Straits of Mackinac.

It is where Lake Huron and Lake Michigan meet under the Mackinac Bridge.

Blue is the color of the endless sky and water

...that surround the eight mile perimeter of the Island.

Blue is the color of the Michigan State Trooper's uniform.

Two troopers work on the Island during the summer.

INDIGO

Indigo is the color of the evening water

...when the last ferry leaves
the Island until the next day.

Indigo is the color of ferry boat hulls.

STAR LINE

RADISSON

Ferry boats take you to Mackinac Island.

Indigo is the color of the twilight sky

...when the Mackinac Bridge lights up for the night.

VIOLET

Violet is the color of lilacs.

Some of the flowering shrubs
are over 200 years old.

Violet is the color that adorns the boats and the floats

...in the Lilac Parade held every June.

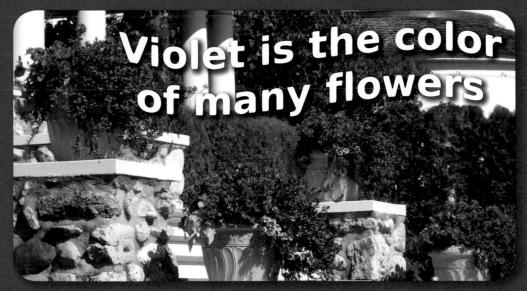

Violet is the color of many flowers

...found in cottage gardens and planters.

BROWN

Brown is the most common color of the 500 Island horses.

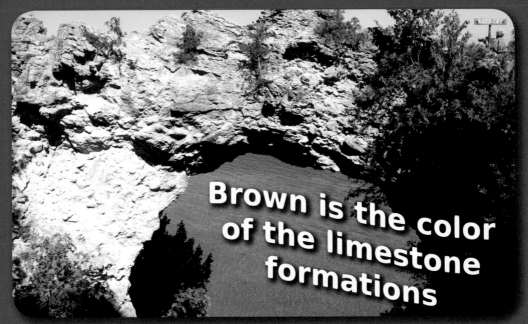

Brown is the color of the limestone formations

...such as Sugar Loaf and Arch Rock.

Brown is the color of fudge,

Plain chocolate is the most popular flavor.

GRAY

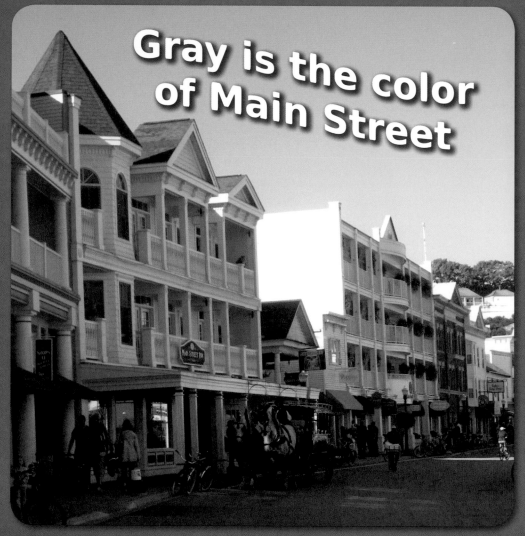

Gray is the color of Main Street

...where many shops offer food, clothes, souvenirs, and fudge!

Gray is the color of a rainy day

...when a rainbow can appear over the Mackinac Bridge.

BLACK

Black is the color
of hitching posts
...that keep the horses secured.

Black is the color of the cannons at Fort Mackinac.

You can hear the cannon blast
several times each day.

**Black is the color
of bicycle tires.**

You can rent a bicycle and
ride around the Island.

WHITE

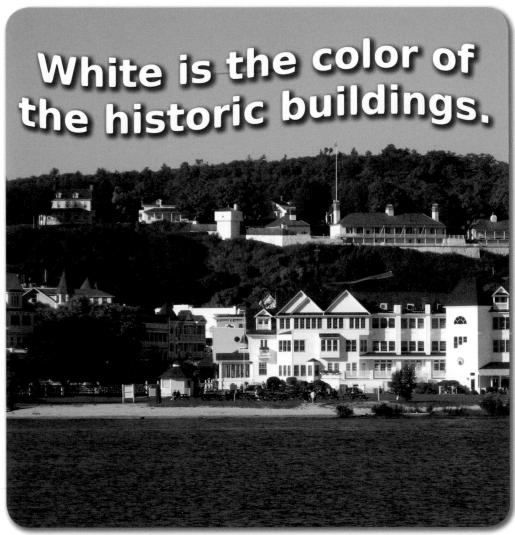

White is the color of the historic buildings.

Visiting Mackinac Island is like
stepping back in time.

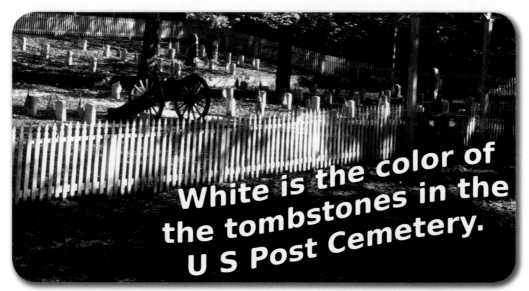

White is the color of the tombstones in the U S Post Cemetery.

The oldest sites date back to the 1820s.

White is the color of Grand Hotel.

More than 130,000 guests stay at Grand Hotel each year.

Come visit
Mackinac
Island and
see if you
can find all
the colors in
the rainbow.

FUDGE RECIPE

12 ounces of semi-sweet chocolate chips
1 can of sweetened condensed milk
1 1/4 powdered sugar
1 tsp vanilla
dash of salt

Melt chocolate chips and milk together on low heat. Once melted, stir in remaining ingredients. Spread evenly into an 8" x 8" buttered pan or line with wax paper. Chill 2–3 hours before serving. Cut into squares after firm. Fudge can be frozen or left at room temperature.

ABOUT THE AUTHOR

Jennifer Margaret Powell has a lifelong love of art, education and the outdoors.

She has worked, lived, and experienced **Mackinac Island** and the **Straits of Mackinac** most of her adult life. Jennifer has a BA in education from Michigan State University and an MA from Eastern Michigan University. This is her second Mackinac Island book. Jennifer lives in Mackinac County with her husband, two sons, and never enough pets. Her favorite color is **blue**.

MACKINAC ISLAND